BEDS AND BEDDING

by

Mary Gordon Watson

Illustrations by

Carole Vincer

THRESHOLD BOOKS

First published in Great Britain by
Threshold Books Ltd, 661 Fulham Road,
London SW6 5PZ

© Threshold Books Ltd 1988

Typeset by Rapid Communications Ltd,
London WC1

Printed in England by Westway Offset

British Library Cataloguing in Publication Data

Beds and bedding.
1. Livestock. Horses. Crafts. Manuals.
I Title   II Vincer, Carole.
636.1′083

ISBN 0-901366-27-7

CONTENTS

Introduction

We confine horses and ponies in stables or stalls mainly for our own convenience.

Most of them adapt well to a 'domesticated' life, preferring to be kept well-fed, dry and warm in winter, and away from insects and hot sun in summer. The more delicate, finer breeds, with less resistance, are no longer accustomed to harsh outdoor conditions. Many others, however, are unhappy if they have to spend up to twenty-four hours in a day shut up in a stable, unable to enjoy the freedom which is natural to them.

It is our duty to make the life of a stabled horse or pony as comfortable and attractive to him as possible. Without clean, fresh conditions and plentiful bedding, he will not thrive physically or mentally.

The most important factors of good bedding will be the method of bedding, the type of flooring and drainage used, the choice of bedding material, and their care and maintenance.

It is hoped that this book will help you to provide your horse with the best possible conditions to keep him healthy and happy in his stable.

Reasons for Bedding

It is often more practical to keep your horse or pony in a stable than turned out in a field, especially when there is no suitable pasture available.

A horse which is ridden every day needs regular feeding and grooming too. It is much easier to keep him in good, fit condition if he is stabled, and if he is wearing hind shoes it could be risky to turn him out with other horses that he might kick.

In winter, most horses need protection against very cold, wet weather, and muddy ground. A warm horse keeps in better condition and needs less food.

In summer, horses may be stabled during the day, to avoid the heat and flies.

When a horse is ill or lame and needs special attention and rest it is far easier to treat him and to monitor his health and feeding if he is stabled. In-foal mares, weaned foals, and youngstock will benefit for the same reasons.

Some form of bedding is necessary for a stabled horse. It encourages him to lie down so that he may rest or sleep, and also to stale. Bedding helps to keep him warm and protects him from draughts. It cushions his legs against the jar of a hard floor, or possible injury such as bruising, capped hocks, or a capped elbow. It will absorb moisture and lessen the effects of urine and manure odours which attract parasites and possible disease.

Most bedding helps to keep horses clean and dry. Indirectly it can also save on food bills. A warm, contented horse stabled on clean, dry, thick bedding will need less food.

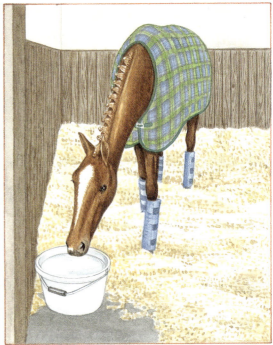

The Stable

A healthy stable must be dry, well ventilated, and well drained. Damp or draughty conditions may cause colds, and could damage the feet and joints, while a stuffy or foul-smelling stable often leads to respiratory or bronchial problems.

The horse should have enough space to move about easily. A loose box 10 ft × 10 ft (3 m × 3 m) is adequate for a pony, but a horse needs 12 ft × 12 ft (4 m × 4 m) to lie down and stretch out if he wants, or roll, without much risk of becoming 'cast'. A foaling box should be 16 ft × 12 ft (5.5 m × 4 m) or larger.

A sound floor surface laid on dry foundations is most important. It must be non-slippery, level and hard wearing. One of the best materials is asphalt. This can be laid over coarse rubble topped with finer gravel to allow natural drainage. Concrete is cheaper and easy to lay, but can be slippery, cold, and jarring. Its surface must always be grooved or roughened. Unless it is very dense and durable, a concrete floor will not last long. Special interlocking, perforated plastic tiles (for straw beds only) can be laid over a concrete, gravel or earthen base. Stable bricks, tiles, or stone slabs must also be extremely tough; otherwise they will chip and break up.

A natural earth floor, or earth base, works well in dry, free-draining situations.

A covered yard or large shed is ideal for stabling more than one horse together, and a deep-litter bedding system will be the most economical. It is specially suitable for youngstock, or horses which need feeding and warmth or occasional exercise.

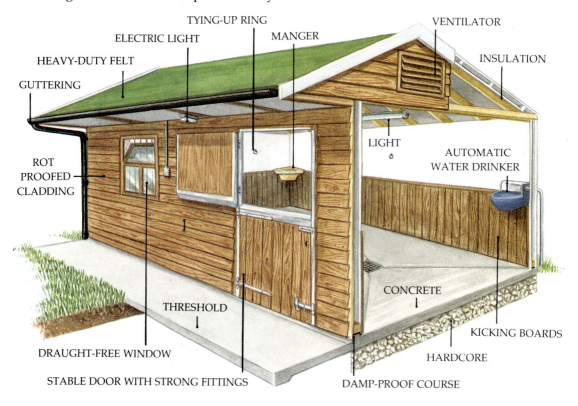

TYING-UP RING

ELECTRIC LIGHT

MANGER

VENTILATOR

HEAVY-DUTY FELT

INSULATION

GUTTERING

LIGHT

AUTOMATIC WATER DRINKER

ROT PROOFED CLADDING

THRESHOLD

CONCRETE

DRAUGHT-FREE WINDOW

KICKING BOARDS

STABLE DOOR WITH STRONG FITTINGS

HARDCORE

DAMP-PROOF COURSE

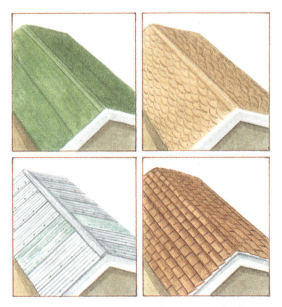

Roofing, lined with wood (not metal): Green roofing felt. Felt slates. Corrugated metal sheeting, with sections of transparent PVC to let in light. Tiles, or slates.

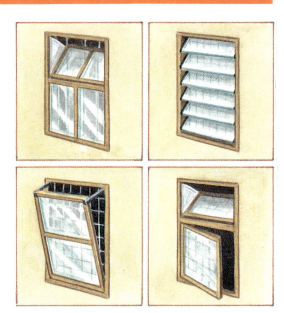

Ventilation Horses need light, and a stable remains healthier and smells better if fresh air is allowed to circulate, and gases and odours can escape.

Floors Concrete (roughened, or grooved). Brick tiles. Perforated plastic/rubber. Asphalt, showing foundations of gravel over a rubble base.

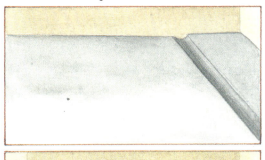

Drainage Good drainage saves extra bedding and helps to keep the air fresh. Shallow, open drains are safer and easier to keep clean and unblocked.

Principles of a Good Bed

Whatever type of bedding is used, it must be dry, soft, clean and fresh. A good bed is warm yet does not overheat in hot conditions or when soiled, and is not harmful if eaten by a horse. It should either absorb liquids and gases, or allow them to reach an outlet for escape.

Straw is the least absorbent bedding, which makes a drainage system necessary. Wood shavings are less absorbent than sawdust, peat or paper.

The choice of bedding material will depend on the amount required and its cost, and how easy it is to obtain and dispose of it. It must also, of course, be suitable for the particular horse or pony. A horse that eats his bedding, for instance, should avoid straw. He will need an inedible, dust-free bed such as paper or good quality wood shavings. Some horses may be allergic to the spores or chemicals found in straw, while others may suffer skin irritation.

Having decided on what bedding to use, it is often less expensive to share a bulk order with others.

The most economical system of bedding is deep-litter. About twelve looseboxes can be skipped out and topped up with clean bedding in the time it takes to muck out one box thoroughly. However, horses produce about eight droppings in twenty-four hours, and unless these are removed frequently and a fresh layer of bedding added, a stable can soon become unhealthy and attract vermin. A good deep-litter bed feels firm yet springy; it must never squelch, or smell.

Alternatively, a semi-deep-litter system could be used when time is short, maintaining only the top surface during the week, but then cleaning out the stable thoroughly at the weekend.

Straw

Straw is a natural and traditional choice of bedding in farming areas where is it easy to obtain.

Wheat straw is by far the best. It is light, yet durable, and the least edible. It should be free of weeds and grass, and not dusty.

Avoid straw containing harmful chemicals, or any which has been so crushed that it becomes too absorbent and less economical. Old straw that has been well stored is drier and crisper than new straw.

When a straw bed is thoroughly shaken out, it is light, airy, and comfortable, and fluid will drain through it.

Oat straw is less durable and horses will eat it. *Barley* straw is also unsuitable: it is prickly, causing skin irritation and possibly colic if eaten.

Bales vary in size and content, so that weight is the only reliable guide to quantity. Use a knife or scissors to cut them open.

Wheat straw

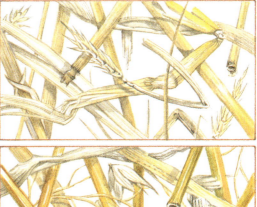

Barley straw (*above*) **Oat straw** (*below*)

Alternative Bedding

Shredded or diced *paper* bedding is ideal to prevent allergies to dust, chemicals or spores. It is extremely absorbent and needs constant renewal.

Sawdust, peat moss, and tan or bark are economical when easily available, but they retain heat and moisture which can damage horses' feet, and *must be kept clean*.

Sawdust is dusty, but is light and easy to work with. Dry, well-seasoned wood is best. *Wood shavings*, or *chips*, cost more but they are less dusty, drain better, and they are convenient to handle, especially when baled.

Peat is heavy, and expensive. It can be damp and cold in winter, hot and dusty in summer, but there is no fire risk.

Bark or *tan* is rarely used, being uncomfortable and damp.

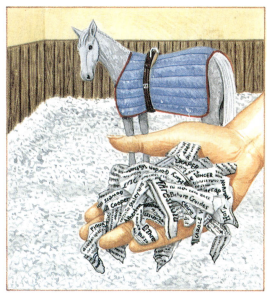

Paper, diced or shredded. Available in bags or compressed in bales.

Wood shavings.

(*above*) **Peat moss**. (*left*) **Tan**. (*right*) **Bark**.

Mucking Out Tools and Equipment

The equipment needed for mucking out will depend on the type of bedding used and the number of horses stabled.

A large, light barrow will be a time- and labour-saving investment. A two-wheeler is easier to balance and steer when full than a single wheelbarrow.

Brooms should be wide and strong, with natural bristle.

A two-prong pitchfork is used for shaking out and bedding down a straw bed.

Manure forks have four prongs, for sorting out straw, and up to ten prongs for sifting finer types of bedding.

A shovel and a rake are needed for shavings, sawdust and peat beds.

Rubber gloves are useful for 'skipping out' into a lightweight container or on to a plastic or hessian muck sheet.

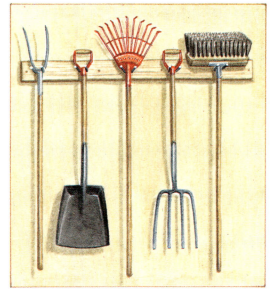

Two-prong pitch fork, shovel, rake, four-prong muck fork and broom.

LARGE BARROW

SINGLE WHEELBARROW

SKIP

PLASTIC BUCKETS

PLASTIC MUCK SHEET

RUBBER GLOVES

LAUNDRY-BASKET/SKIP

Mucking Out a Straw Bed

The task of mucking out will be considerably easier if droppings are picked up frequently. The longer they are left, the more they are spread around, soiling large areas of bedding. It also helps to keep the horse cleaner, his feet healthier, and the air fresher, at the same time keeps flies, worms and disease at bay.

A sparse, thin bed is *not* an economy. Urine will be absorbed over a wider area, and most of the bedding will soon become soiled so that all of it will have to be removed.

Although initially a larger amount of bedding is required to lay a thick bed, if tended regularly it will need little topping up and the horse should stay safer and healthier.

Remove haynet and buckets. Pick up all visible droppings, then shake out the straw so that the heavier, soiled bedding falls through the prongs.

Separate the clean straw and throw it in the cleanest corner or against the back wall, leaving the soiled bedding piled near the door.

Fork the remaining muck into the barrow. Slightly soiled bedding can be spread in another corner or outside the door, to aerate and dry.

Sweep the floor well and pick up any remaining muck using the broom and shovel, then empty the barrow and leave the floor bare until it has dried out.

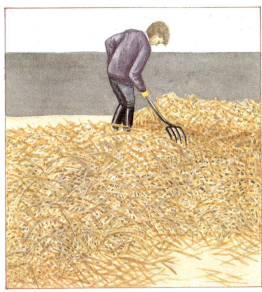

Bank up the bedding in the corners and around the edges with fresh straw, to help to protect horses from injury, and to get up again, if they lie down and roll.

Use a pitchfork to shake and spread out the used clean bedding. It will make a less slippery base than the fresh straw which is then added on top and at the sides.

A clean, deep, level straw bed will help to make the unnatural life of a stabled horse as safe, healthy and comfortable as he deserves.

Mucking Out Other Types of Bedding ■

It is always important to remove droppings regularly, whether the stable is cleaned out thoroughly every day or a deep-litter method is used.

Wood shavings, sawdust, paper, or peat bedding can be skipped out quickly using rubber gloves and a lightweight container or muck sheet. Very wet patches must also be removed. The depth should be maintained to allow urine to drain below the surface and the horse to get up and down without scraping the floor. Slightly damp bedding can be left undisturbed as a non-slippery base.

Deep littering saves energy and expense but droppings *must* be removed frequently and new bedding added. Whenever a stable becomes soggy, smelly, or too deep, the entire contents should be dug out, and the floor cleaned, aired and left to dry.

Shavings Use a shavings fork or a shovel to remove droppings and wet patches. Level with a rake, then add a layer of fresh shavings, banked up at the sides.

Paper A paper bed must be at least 4 ins (10 cm) deep. Pick up droppings with a fork or by hand, and remove soggy areas. Damp bedding should be turned and aired.

Peat Remove droppings with a shovel or close-pronged fork (they can be hard to find), and dig out very wet bedding. Rake the surface to loosen and aerate it.

Mucking Out with a Horse in the Stable

It is much easier to muck out an empty stable. If this is not possible, first tie up the horse or pony. The door can then be left open. However quiet and well behaved he may be, this is safer because you know exactly where he is, and if something suddenly startles him, he cannot trample or barge you, or escape through the door.

Muck out *carefully* around him—a puncture wound from a dirty fork prong can become seriously infected. Move the horse over when you need to clean the area where he has been standing.

Pile up the used, clean bedding around the sides.

Pick out the horse's feet directly into a skip or on to the bare stable floor, before sweeping up any remaining dirt. Then leave the floor to dry out, if time allows, before bedding down. Once again, be extremely careful if using a pitchfork.

When mucking out with a horse in the stable, tie him up securely to a strong wall fixture, using a quick-release knot.

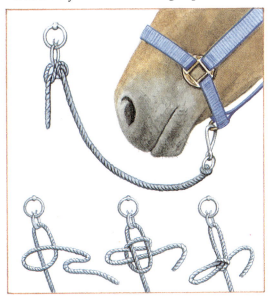

Use a well-fitting headcollar or halter, with a rope attached to the rear D-ring, and tie him up to a loop of breakable string as a safety precaution.

Never leave mucking-out equipment where a horse could injure himself on it, and never leave him loose on a bare, slippery floor.

The Muck Heap

A muck heap should be convenient for emptying barrows or muck sheets, and easily accessible for disposal vehicles. Ideally it should be possible to tip muck down on to it (soiled bedding is extremely heavy to throw upwards), and preferably out of sight to avoid the odours and flies.

Small muck heaps close to stables should be emptied regularly. Larger or long-term heaps for rotting manure may be compressed tightly for quicker decomposition, and to generate heat, which will discourage flies from breeding.

Gardeners like straw and peat manure, but sawdust and shavings take longer to rot down and disposal can be difficult. Paper waste may be burned.

Used shavings can improve muddy gateways or standing areas, and will soften up hard or rutted riding tracks.

A builder's skip or flat trailer has the advantage of being portable and may be provided and removed by a muck dealer. A ramp would aid unloading.

A simple pen can be constructed using posts and wire netting, or corrugated iron or similar materials, although muck disposal might prove more difficult.

A permanent walled-in muck heap must be sited to allow a vehicle fitted with a 'grabber' attachment to park alongside so as to empty it.

Old sacks can be used to bag up droppings, which are popular for garden use (very little bedding should be included), and it is cheaper than commercial fertilisers.

If there is local demand for it, straw manure (mainly droppings) can be unloaded straight into a **muck spreader**, which will then be used to fertilise fields.

Fresh, rather than rotted manure, is favoured by mushroom growers who need to cultivate under ideal conditions, as in the method shown above.

Horse manure is traditionally the most suitable fertiliser for growing roses. It also benefits young trees, and innumerable other plants, shrubs and vegetables.

Bad Stable Habits

Most horses would prefer to live out in a field, at least for part of the time, than to spend up to twenty-four hours per day confined in a stable.

Many stable vices develop because of lack of exercise, or the wrong diet, but sometimes dirty, inadequate bedding is to blame. A good, deep bed can prevent kicking, stamping or continual pawing of the floor.

If a horse eats his bed it should be sprinkled with a disinfectant which is not harmful if eaten, or inedible bedding used instead. Alternatively, the horse must be tied up, muzzled or restrained with crossed side-reins for part of the day. The problem becomes far more serious if the horse eats his own droppings. The same remedies should be tried, but in bad cases a strong worm-control programme and special diet will be necessary.

Stamping and pawing.

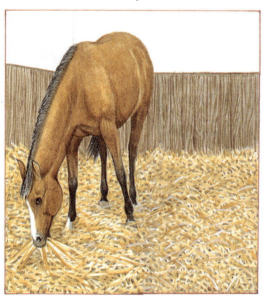

Bed eating.

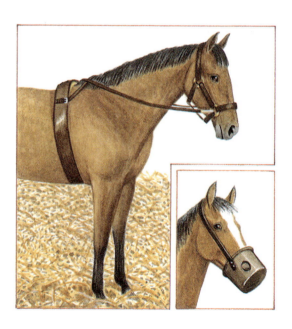

A muzzle or **crossed side-reins** will prevent a horse eating his bed.

Dealing with a Cast Horse

A horse is said to be 'cast' when he cannot get to his feet because he is lying jammed against a wall, or in a corner, or under a manger. He will often panic and kick frantically, and might injure himself seriously. Some horses will lie quietly and wait to be rescued.

Scratchy, prickly bedding (or rugs) can cause a horse to roll violently. If the sides of the bed are well banked up—particularly at night when he is likely to lie down—and if he wears an anti-cast roller, it should prevent him getting into this jam.

It may be possible to slide him clear of the obstruction, but great care is needed to avoid being kicked. If not, one person should hold down his head to keep him still, while another loops a lungeing rein around his legs, to roll him right over. He will then get up on his own.

A horse cast against a stable wall.

Using a lunge rein to roll him over.

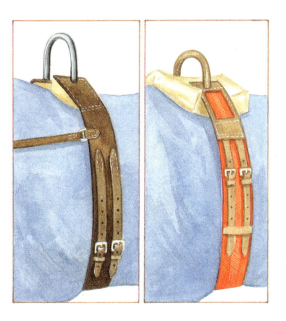

Two types of anti-cast roller.

Some Stable Ailments

Stabled horses, like those at grass, need a regular worm dose. Droppings, which contain the eggs and larvae of various types of *worms*, will re-infest them, and could cause severe and lasting internal damage. Red worm is the most common; it is almost invisible, yet large numbers can destroy the bowel lining and sometimes blood vessels too.

Diseases can spread through stables rapidly. A horse with a contagious skin disease, such as *ringworm*, should be isolated. His used bedding should be burned and the stable thoroughly disinfected. The same precautions are necessary if *coughing* or *influenza* breaks out.

Thrush is a fungal infection of the horse's heel and frog, usually caused by standing on wet bedding in a dirty or poorly drained stable. It smells very unpleasant.

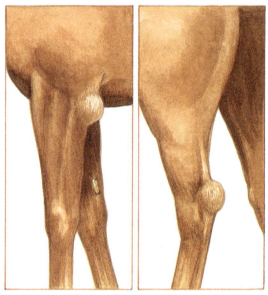

Capped elbow (*left*), and **capped hock** (*right*), are soft swellings, often the result of a blow or abrasion due to lack of bedding in the stable.

Some horses are allergic to straw, spores, or dust, and will **cough** when stabled. They need an alternative type of bedding and plenty of fresh air.

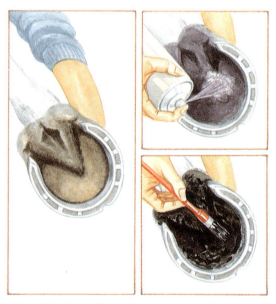

A healthy foot (*left*). Treatment of **thrush** (*right*) with an antibiotic spray (*above*), and an application of Stockholm tar (*below*).

Hygiene

No-one really likes mucking out or sweeping up, but a clean, well-managed stable is essential for the health of the horse.

Dung will harbour worms and attract flies and parasites, while rats and mice will also thrive on it; they especially enjoy filthy drains.

A pressure hose used with a suitable cleaning agent is very effective for disinfecting stable floors and drains, particularly after an infectious disease, after foaling, or after a deep-litter bed has been cleaned out.

- Always pick up all droppings, whichever mucking-out system is used.
- Keep the muck heap in a suitable place—preferably downwind—and empty it often.
- Employ an expert to keep down vermin—or a good stable cat.
- Keep drains clean and disinfected.

The area surrounding a stable needs to be kept clean so that insects, vermin and germs are not invited, and the air remains pure and fresh.

A high-pressure hose can be used with various attachments to spray heavily soiled floors and walls with detergent or disinfectant.

After cleaning stables and drains a disinfectant will help to kill germs and maintain healthy conditions for a longer period. It should also deter vermin.

Safety

- *NEVER* allow smoking in the stable area.
- All electrical fittings must be checked regularly by a qualified electrician.
- Avoid using highly inflammatory materials, like petrol or gas, in or near a stable.
- *Never* leave a stable door unbolted unless the horse is tied up.
- Use a quick-release knot to tie up a horse. Tie him to a piece of breakable string in case he pulls back and panics.
- *Never* leave mucking-out tools in the stable, *nor* leaning near the door where he could chew them, *nor* lying about as a hazard to horse or person.
- Don't leave loose baler twine about—it might tangle around legs, choke a horse if eaten, or snarl up machinery.
- *Never* leave a horse loose on a bare, slippery floor.

Anti-fire regulations must be strictly obeyed. Fire extinguishers and a hose are necessary equipment—and *NO SMOKING!*

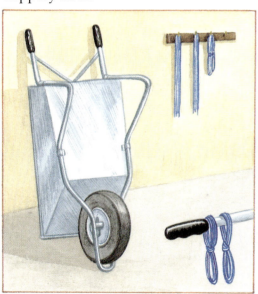

Park the barrow safely out of the way—under cover or tipped up to keep dry. Save baler twine for making ropes, haynets, or other useful items.

Loose, flapping clothes can startle a horse. They also hamper movement and efficiency. Flat, non-slip shoes or boots are best.

Storage

All bedding should be kept in dry, airy conditions.

A spare stable or shed will do well if it is damp-proof.

A large covered barn with open sides is suitable for storage, but remember that straw will be ruined if it gets very wet. The bottom bales should be stacked on top of wooden pallets if conditions might be damp.

Polythene-wrapped bales of wood-shavings, peat or paper can be stacked outside, but they are likely to get damp and need at least a tarpaulin cover. A lean-to shed or shelter is easy to erect.

As a rough guide, about 2 tons/ tonnes of straw (approximately 100 bales) should last a stabled horse from October to March.

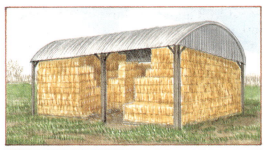

(*above*) Large barn, agricultural Dutch style. (*below*) Barn, enclosed on at least three sides.

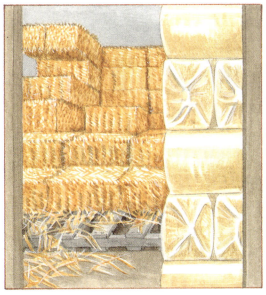

Spare stable, or shed, with bales stacked on top of pallets to keep them dry and aerated.

(*above*) Heavy-duty tarpaulin cover, weighted down. (*below*) A basic lean-to shed with sloping roof and guttering.

Points to Remember

Well laid-out stabling saves time and energy if it allows you to keep it clean and care for the horse efficiently with minimum effort.

No matter how good the quality of bedding, it becomes useless unless the following points are borne in mind.

The bedding should be:

CLEAN—dirty bedding makes a stable unhealthy and smell unpleasant, which will affect the horse's health and comfort.

PLENTIFUL—to keep the horse warm, and protect him against injury. It will encourage him to lie down safely, and to stale—the urine will be better absorbed.

The stable should be:

DRY—with free drainage, never liable to flood. A stable with doors and windows exposed to driving rain is not suitable in wet conditions, but good ventilation for fresh air is essential. On a damp or boggy site, the floor should be raised and drain away well to a reliable outlet.

SAFE—large enough to move about easily, and to lie down without being trapped. The floor must be level and not slippery.